COAC

D0482837

SUCCESSFULLY

JOHN EATON
AND ROY JOHNSON

A Dorling Kindersley Book

LONDON, NEW YORK, MUNICH,
MELBOURNE, DELHI

Managing Editor Adèle Hayward
Senior Designer Jamie Hanson
DTP Designers Julian Dams, Amanda Peers
Production Controller Michelle Thomas

Senior Managing Editor Stephanie Jackson
Senior Managing Art Editor Nigel Duffield
US Editors Gary Werner, Margaret Parrish

Produced for Dorling Kindersley by

studio **cactus** ©

13 SOUTHGATE STREET WINCHESTER HAMPSHIRE SO23 9DZ

Editor Kate Hayward
Designer Laura Watson

First American Edition, 2000
04 05 10 9 8 7 6 5 4

Published in the United States by
Dorling Kindersley Publishing, Inc.
375 Hudson Street New York, NY 10014

Library of Congress Cataloging-in-Publication Data

Johnson, Roy, 1944–
Coaching successfully / Roy Johnson and John Eaton
    p. cm.-- (Essential managers)
Includes index.
ISBN 0-7894-7147-7 (alk. paper)
1. Leadership. 2. Employee motivation.
I. Eaton, John, 1956– II. Title. III. Series.

HD57.7 J644 2001
658.3'124--dc21
                                    00-047415

Reproduced by Colourscan, Singapore
Printed in China by WKT

See our complete catalog at
www.dk.com

CONTENTS

MAKING COACHING WORK

REFINING COACHING

INTRODUCTION

The ability to raise the performance of your staff and seek long-term goals for them to work toward is an important element of being a good manager. Through coaching, you can develop staff to take on more responsibility and give yourself more time to get on with the job of managing. Coaching Successfully will help you get the best from your team and let you focus on achieving better results for your organization. Practical advice, including 101 concise tips, shows you how to develop the coaching approach in yourself and others, and a self-assessment test at the end of the book allows you to evaluate your skills as a coach. As you seek to instil coaching values in those around you, this book will be an invaluable source of reference and advice.

UNDERSTANDING COACHING

Coaching helps you bring out the potential of your staff. Use it to deal with immediate problems, as a constructive way to interact with your staff, and as an aid to their long-term development.

WHAT IS COACHING?

Coaching is the art of improving the performance of others. Managers who coach encourage their teams to learn from and be challenged by their work. Create the conditions for continuous development by helping your staff to define and achieve goals.

I Use coaching to develop skills and talents in your team.

▲ COACHING QUALITIES
A good coach listens first, asks searching questions, provides constructive feedback, and is ready to generate creative ideas.

HOW COACHING WORKS

The coaching process closes the gap between an individual's or team's present level of performance and the desired one. This can happen within a single coaching session, or over a long cycle of sessions. As a coach, you will help develop your employees by mutually assessing performance, discussing the present situation, defining achievable goals, exploring new initiatives, and supporting a coachee in their plan of action. Coaching refers both to specific interacting skills – used both in everyday situations and in more structured meetings – and the encouragement of long-term learning.

STRUCTURING COACHING

DEFINITION
Determine performance goals

ANALYSIS
Understand the present reality

EXPLORATION
Explore options to achieve goals

ACTION
Say when tasks will be done

LEARNING
Implement agreed upon actions

FEEDBACK
Review progress at next session

THE COACHING PROCESS

Coaching is an unending process – each new achievement forms a platform for the next challenge. However, for any one coaching goal there is a cycle of six basic stages from goal to completion. First, the coach and employee agree what the goals of coaching are; second, they discuss the present position; third, they explore the available options; and fourth, they identify and commit to a course of action. These steps can often be completed in a single coaching session. The coachee then implements the agreed upon action with the support of the coach, and with a view to permanently raising performance levels. In the final stage, the coach and coachee hold the next coaching session and consider what has been learned and how this learning can be built upon.

2 Use the final stage of a coaching cycle to initiate the next cycle by defining the next achievable goal.

COACHING FUNDAMENTALS

It is not necessary to know everything about your employee's work to coach them well. In fact, much good coaching occurs when the manager is able to take an objective view of an employee's goals without being distracted by details. Good coaches help employees learn from their mistakes, identify their performance targets, and take responsibility for implementing the first step. As a coach, avoid trying to tell people what to do, but, instead, help them choose the best route to succeed in their objectives. Use coaching to teach your employees to adopt a positive approach to learning by encouraging them to say what they think.

POINTS TO REMEMBER

● If your team has a positive attitude, it is more able to face new challenges.

● A good coach encourages a team to discuss their ideas.

● Staff should have the necessary resources to achieve their goals.

3 Encourage staff to come to their own conclusions.

WHY COACH?

By coaching, managers release their own time, improve their staff's performance, and enhance the productivity of their organizations. Coach and delegate more, and supervise less, to boost productivity and help team members fulfill their potential.

4 Invest in people in the short term, and reap the benefits in the long term.

YOU CAN DELEGATE

You hand over more responsibility

Trust is established

Staff skills are increased

You do take time to coach

DELEGATING MORE

Managers with their eye on future success use coaching to develop skill and positive attitudes in their staff. It takes effort to maintain performance, let alone improve it, so be prepared to invest time in people's development. Once you have confidence in your staff's skills, and have developed a good relationship built on trust, you can begin to delegate some of your responsibilities to them.

◀ **UPWARD SPIRAL OF RESPONSIBILITY**
Investing time in improving the skill and confidence of your staff leads to an upward spiral of events, when you can delegate projects and get on with focusing on long-term managerial issues.

SUPERVISING LESS

Unless you develop your staff, they will be unable to cope with the responsibilities you want to give them. Coaching provides a solution. Coach your staff to accept their own responsibilities. This eases some of the pressure on you, so that you can focus on your own, longer-term responsibilities. In the meantime, your staff are achieving greater job satisfaction because they are allowed to make their own decisions and achieve independence.

You do not take time to coach

Trust of staff is insufficient

Workload is higher

Stress is increased

YOU CAN'T DELEGATE

DOWNWARD SPIRAL OF DEVELOPMENT ▶
If you do not invest time in developing the skills of your staff, you may need to supervise them to ensure work is done properly. This leads to long hours and stress for you and your staff.

BRINGING OUT POTENTIAL

Asking searching questions and giving constructive feedback will encourage your staff to become more aware of their strengths and weaknesses. Help them to build on their strengths and to develop new skills, so that they can take on new challenges. Coach them to learn from both their successes and mistakes. As their competence and confidence improve, their self-esteem grows, and they will take more initiative in meeting agreed goals. Increasingly, by using all of their abilities and expressing their potential to the full, your whole team will benefit.

5 Use coaching to achieve increased productivity.

6 Identify, encourage, and build on your team's existing strengths and skills.

Coachee takes a confident role in the team; team benefits from shared strengths

THE NEEDS OF THE TEAM
Mutual support and increased skills

Coach benefits from an efficient team; team benefits from the manager focusing on long-term development

THE NEEDS OF THE COACHEE
Job satisfaction and fulfillment

THE NEEDS OF THE COACH
More time to be results focused

◀ **BENEFITS FOR ALL**
The role of the coach is pivotal to the needs of the team. Through coaching, the coachee has the benefit of personal and career development; the team is strengthened by having motivated and skilled staff; and the coach has more time to devote to management and results.

Coach and coachee aim for the same goals

7 Increase fulfillment by delegating responsibility for whole projects.

DO'S AND DON'TS

✔ Do make coaching one of your most important priorities.	✗ Don't delay coaching until there is nothing better to do.
✔ Do develop staff by delegating tasks that stretch their abilities.	✗ Don't just delegate the activities you would prefer not to do.
✔ Do tell staff how coaching works.	✗ Don't be afraid to take time coaching.

INVOLVING PEOPLE

Teams in business need high morale to perform well. Research shows that when people take part in decision making they have greater commitment to the final decision. Engage people in a search for ways of achieving their goals, rather than giving them ready-made answers. Remember that coaching is a two-way process that involves people in the choices that most affect them – in their jobs and their development. Your staff will benefit from the coaching approach because a sense of ownership for decisions is highly motivational.

8 Find out what your team values most in its work.

9 Involve your staff in decisions that affect them.

POINTS TO REMEMBER

- Team members who have been included in decisions feel empowered to achieve more.
- Teams and individuals should learn to recognize and use each other's strengths.
- Each team member should feel they play an essential role in the structure of the team.
- Team members should feel free to contribute their ideas about the team's goals and methods.

DEVELOPING POSITIVE ATTITUDES IN STAFF

When people's self-confidence and motivation grow, they take on more challenging assignments. They prove to themselves that they can handle these challenges, and they are able to solve many of the problems that inevitably arise. They know that if they do run into trouble you, their coach, will support them. This builds a positive attitude to change, and when your staff are presented with further challenges, they are more likely to accept them, rather than to give reasons why they cannot.

CASE STUDY

The subsidiary of one of Europe's biggest food producers had an ambitious goal to double shareholder value every four years. It implemented a decision-making process to evaluate and select products, activities, and markets adding greater value to the business. Their organization development manager recognized, however, that achieving strategic goals ultimately depended on staff –

their understanding, skill, and commitment were required in order to meet the inevitable new challenges. This reflected the chairman's publicized view that achieving strategic goals was 80 percent about people. In order to equip staff with the skills, the management development manager trained and encouraged all line managers to coach their people. The result was the hoped for increase in the productivity of the organization.

◀ **INVESTING IN EMPLOYEES**
In this case study, the director of the organization saw that it was necessary to equip staff with skills to enable them to respond positively to the challenge of new markets and increased competition. Coaching was used to develop the skills and attitudes of staff, which led to an increase in productivity.

INCREASING PRODUCTIVITY

Your team's ability to work efficiently increases as member skills improve through your coaching. The coaching goals you agree on make clear to everyone involved what good performance looks like. With this knowledge, teams can spot and correct mistakes more quickly, and can use their skill to deliver the required quality of work. The result is greater productivity. Just the increased attention coaching brings can improve performance. So, by coaching, you influence staff performance in two ways: first, through their professional development; second, through the positive attention of your coaching.

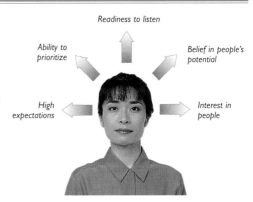

Readiness to listen

Ability to prioritize

Belief in people's potential

High expectations

Interest in people

▲ QUALITIES OF A GOOD COACH

There are a number of important qualities that a coach needs to possess in order to bring out the potential of staff, and in doing so, increase a team's competence and productivity.

10 Agree on clear performance standards so that the team has a level against which to assess itself.

THE HAWTHORNE EXPERIMENT

In the 1920s, physiologist Elton Mayo conducted experiments at the Hawthorne Electrical Works in Chicago. He was attempting to prove his theory that better lighting led to greater productivity. First, Mayo had the lights turned up on the factory floor. As he expected, production levels went up too. Mayo had proven his theory – or had he? As an afterthought, he decided to turn the lights down to see what

would happen. To his surprise, production went up again. He found that whatever he did with the lighting, production went up. Mayo discussed his findings with the workers involved. They said that the interest shown in them by Mayo and his researchers had made them feel more valued. They were used to being ignored. The increase in morale led to an improvement in productivity. This effect is known as the "Hawthorne Effect."

DECIDING TO COACH

There are many applications to coaching. You can initiate coaching yourself or respond to requests for help. Look out for opportunities to coach on such issues as problem solving, career development, lack of motivation, and teamwork.

11 Look for every appropriate opportunity to coach your staff.

BUILDING SKILLS

Job satisfaction requires a continual supply of new goals and challenges to stretch the employee's potential to the utmost. As you prioritize personal development within your team they will naturally seek opportunities to extend their skills. Coaching is a natural follow-up to training. To bring out your team's potential, a combination of training, on-the-job learning, and coaching can be unbeatable.

Staff take steps to new challenges by building on skills learned

NEW GOAL

REVIEW

PRACTICE

COACH

TRAIN

INDUCT

CONSOLIDATING STEPS ▶
Help define step-by-step goals so staff can learn, understand, practice, and review skills before moving on to new challenges.

PROGRESSING PROJECTS

It is part of your role as a manager to delegate responsibility for projects, support staff in their work, and ensure that projects are completed satisfactorily. Coaching is an ideal way to keep individuals on track without undermining their responsibility. Hold coaching meetings over the life of a project so you are able to receive progress reports, troubleshoot problems, and monitor standards. When your staff come to you with difficulties, coach them to find a solution.

SOLVING PROBLEMS

You may be approached by a member of your staff for help, or you may decide that you need to address a performance issue with an individual. Either way, coaching can be used to help find solutions to a problem. This does not mean that you want to become the source of all solutions. If you did that, there would soon be little time to manage. Reduce precious management time spent on firefighting by coaching staff to think through problems for themselves and to come up with their own plan for resolution.

12 Avoid taking over problems from your staff.

13 Use coaching to explore ways of solving problems.

14 Groom your deputy to be ready to take over your projects.

DEFINING MILESTONES ▼
Use coaching to define the employee's next career milestone, give feedback, establish new training needs, and set achievable targets in the pursuit of these goals.

DEVELOPING CAREERS

A sense of career direction is essential if employees are to feel that they are valued by the organization. It is for this reason that regular performance reviews are standard practice in most organizations. The coaching approach can dovetail neatly with reviews, through which you can agree developmental goals with employees and give support while they achieve them. With particularly able staff, coaching can be an ideal way to keep them moving onward and upward.

Coach ▶ **Feedback** ▶ **Set Targets**

OVERCOMING CONFLICTS

Conflicts between individuals, between managers and staff, or between employees and customers are a fact of life. Reduce conflicts within your own team by encouraging openness, responsibility for high standards, and a creative approach to problems. Where your attention is drawn to disagreements, coach to explore the root of the issue and to resolve misunderstanding.

15 Defuse disputes and disagreements by encouraging staff to respect opposing viewpoints.

REMOTIVATING STAFF

Demoralized staff can quickly spread discontent. Often this occurs as a result of poor communication between managers and team members. Improve morale by helping people explore their differences honestly and to look at the causes of current problems. Another reason for a loss of motivation may be that individuals are bored or dissatisfied. When staff come to you expressing dissatisfaction, encourage them to talk openly about the causes of the problem as well as the problem itself. Managers who coach have a means of aligning staff personal goals with the mission of the organization itself.

FOCUSING ON ACHIEVING GOALS ▶
The best performers are focused on what they really want. Look for ways to remotivate dissatisfied staff by exploring their needs, recognizing their aspirations, and establishing new goals.

16 Make it clear that all ideas are worth hearing.

POINTS TO REMEMBER

- Coaching can be used whenever you want to improve performance or increase motivation levels.
- Coaching is not training, although it can help employees implement and practice new skills.
- To find a solution, problems should be looked at from as many points of view as possible.
- Coaching feedback should be specific, factual, and objective.
- New ways for staff advancement should be explored.

BRAINSTORMING

Despite the best efforts of your staff, projects will stall as problems arise from unforeseen difficulties. This can easily lead to a loss of responsibility for the project and a weakening of team spirit – often noticeable when staff start to blame others for delays. Unresolved difficulties can cause frustration or, worse, quick-fixes that solve nothing. When you notice that projects are stalling, or when your team comes to you with setbacks, coach them to move things on by defining the present state of affairs. Consolidate the team by inviting an open contribution of ideas from all team members to come up with possible solutions.

17 Use team coaching to foster mutual learning and support, and to create new initiatives.

DECIDING WHEN AND HOW TO COACH

REASON FOR COACHING	ACTIONS TO TAKE
BUILDING SKILLS Set up opportunities for new skills to be learned and practiced.	● Use coaching to break up large-scale tasks into smaller ones, gradually introducing new skills. ● Before selecting a training program, coach your staff to identify performance targets they want to achieve.
PROGRESSING PROJECTS Oversee progress and monitor any problems on projects.	● Link coaching sessions with progress reports over the life of the project. ● Work through problems that could hinder the successful completion of the project.
SOLVING PROBLEMS Help staff to identify problems and possible routes to a solution.	● Encourage staff to define the problem and to come up with their own route to a solution. ● Remain sympathetic to your staff's difficulties, while encouraging them to deal with problems robustly.
DEVELOPING CAREERS Prepare staff for promotion or show them a clear career path.	● Work on coaching goals that could result in recognition for staff achievements. ● Focus on long-term projects that are challenging and bring out potential, rather than small-scale jobs.
OVERCOMING CONFLICTS Defuse disagreements among team members.	● Coach staff to develop greater insight into others' perspectives and therefore avoid misunderstandings. ● Overcome friction by directing attention to results rather than personalities.
REMOTIVATING STAFF Restore enthusiasm and commitment within the team.	● Establish people's needs and aspirations and link these to performance targets. ● Be prepared to dig for the issues that really concern the employee and be ready to talk through them.
BRAINSTORMING Direct the creative input of the team to keep projects on track.	● Accentuate the generation of creative options rather than getting bogged down in problems. ● In team coaching, take a lead by offering creative ideas of your own, and then invite the team to assess them.

SELECTING A COACHING STYLE

Sometimes people like clear direction and definite answers to their questions. At other times, they want to be involved in a dialogue about their own development and goals. Select the style most appropriate for the coachee and to the objective of coaching.

18 Be ready to adapt your coaching style during a coaching session.

19 Ask questions and listen to the coachee, but also offer ideas and teach skills if necessary.

USING "PUSH" AND "PULL"

There is a spectrum of coaching styles ranging from "push" at one extreme to "pull" at the other. "Push" is akin to instruction. You give the coachee clear answers or show them how to perform a skill. At the opposite end of the spectrum is "pull," where you draw out a coachee's existing strengths. In the first style, you do most of the talking, while in the second, you do most of the listening. Both styles are used in coaching, and a skilled coach can move effortlessly between the two.

ADAPTING YOUR STYLE

"Push" style coaching can be useful in the early stages of a person's development, when they lack confidence and competence. The advantages of "push" are that it is quick and provides answers, teaching procedures step-by-step. The problem is that it leads to dependence on you for the answers to problems. Using the "pull" style, act as a catalyst to help staff find their own answers. Listen to answers and then probe further to help coachees create their own solutions. Such an approach results in coachees feeling accountable for results and being able to take the initiative.

POINTS TO REMEMBER

- "Pull" style coaching can irritate people who are used to being spoon-fed answers.
- "Pull" style coaching takes more time and more skill as a coach, but the benefits in terms of staff commitment are well worth it.
- If coachees develop their own solutions, they feel more motivated to achieve goals.
- If you use the "push" style, be sure that the coachee is able to reproduce the skill or procedure.

Coach does most talking

Coachee is quiet and dependent

Coach sees that coachee is ready to take initiative

Coachee is self-reliant and confident

Coach encourages and listens

PUSH **TRANSITION** **PULL**

CHANGING STYLES ▲

Match your coaching style to the motivation and skill level of your staff. Use a "pull" style as much as possible. Reserve a "push" style for those with low skill and low self-reliance, but change over to a "pull" style as they gain in confidence.

20 Introduce the "pull" style of coaching by asking more questions than you answer.

ADAPTING AN EMPLOYEE'S MOTIVATION LEVEL

LOW WILL/LOW SKILL

- "Pull" for coachee's reasons for being in the job. Find a motivational need and link learning to its fulfillment.

- "Push" to give plenty of direction and be ready to provide time and support.

LOW WILL/HIGH SKILL

- "Pull" to find motivational needs and aspirations, and find ways to focus on new challenges and goals.

- "Pull" to find if the employee is being stretched. Begin to establish trust.

HIGH WILL/LOW SKILL

- "Push" and give directions at first, then ease off and encourage the employee to find their own way.

- "Push" to teach new skills and set achievable goals to build confidence.

HIGH WILL/HIGH SKILL

- "Pull" by identifying challenges that provide opportunities for personal and career development.

- "Pull" by listening to the coachee's assessment, ideas, and options.

EMOTIONAL INTELLIGENCE AND COACHING

Top performers are distinguished by their self-motivation, self-awareness, self-regulation, and ability to influence others. These qualities are known as "emotional intelligence." Work on developing these qualities in yourself and in your staff.

21 Encourage your staff to analyze their own strengths and weaknesses.

22 Help people gain good relationship skills such as empathy and sensitivity.

WHAT IS EMOTIONAL INTELLIGENCE?

According to Daniel Goleman's theory, success in business depends on emotional intelligence rather than academic learning. People with emotional intelligence are self-aware, self-regulated, and motivated. They are sensitive to others' feelings and have the ability to influence people. Be a successful coach by developing these qualities in yourself and in others.

BEING AWARE

People who are self-aware know how they feel and how they are likely to react. They know that anger caused by an incident in one meeting can pollute the next if they do not discharge the bad feeling. Recognize and develop your own strengths: look for assignments that you will excel at. Seek coaching for areas you need improvement in. Self-awareness will enable you to make the best use of your skills.

QUESTIONS TO ASK YOURSELF

Q Am I aware of my limitations?

Q When do I take the time to analyze my own strengths and weaknesses?

Q Do I play to my strengths and develop skills in areas I am gifted in?

Q Do I know which times of the day I am able to work to my full potential?

Q Do I take a break when I feel jaded and unmotivated?

Q Do I delegate tasks to staff when I know they will get a better result than I will?

Q What important tasks can I reserve for the time of day I am most alert?

Q Am I able to see how my behavior can affect others?

REMAINING IN CONTROL

Self-regulation is the ability to accept and manage one's feelings. It goes hand in hand with self-awareness. Emotionally intelligent people work well within teams and develop good working relationships. Be aware of your nerves before a meeting. Call on memories of past success to trigger the necessary confidence for a task at hand. When conflicts arise, remain in control by analyzing your own reactions and responding appropriately, and encourage staff to do the same.

23 Persuade staff to overcome setbacks by focusing on past achievements.

24 Encourage staff to predict, and be prepared for, possible problems.

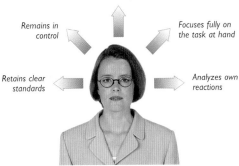

Recalls past successes to boost confidence

Remains in control

Focuses fully on the task at hand

Retains clear standards

Analyzes own reactions

◀ **EMOTIONAL AWARENESS**
A self-regulated person is able to focus fully on a goal. He or she has clear standards, but recognizes limitations and knows that he or she may need to take time out from a busy schedule in order to rejuvenate.

REMAIN FOCUSED ▶
Strong commitment to his goals, and an ability to remain focused were a deciding factor in the success of a top car-salesperson. His concentration on the task at hand was sharper and more consistent than that of his colleagues. His emotional intelligence meant he was also able to foster and retain good working relationships.

CASE STUDY
A salesperson in a car dealership exhibited a stronger ability to focus on a goal than his colleagues in the office. He remained able to manage his workload and was not distracted by things happening around him. This was most obvious when his colleagues chattered idly around his desk. He continued to make phone calls to follow up sales leads despite the distraction. In that year, he sold more than twice as many cars as the next best performing salesperson. At the same time, he was sociable and had a good working relationship with his colleagues and clients. However, his self-regulation meant that he spent more time than others working on the highest sales priorities, such as prospecting for sales, following up client meetings, and customer service. Consistently performing to his own high standards, he went on to become one of the car manufacturer's star performers.

UNDERSTANDING MOTIVATIONAL NEEDS

Feeling motivated is having the desire to excel for oneself and for the organization. Although high performers have a burning desire to be at the top of the ladder, they work within the interests of the organization. This gives them their long-term success, and is why their organizations value them highly. Link your own and your staff's desire to succeed with the motivation to continually seek new ways to improve your organization's service.

THINGS TO DO

1. Match personal priorities to those of the organization.

2. Learn from setbacks, rather than be defeated by them.

3. Focus on remaining positive and ahead of the game.

25 Motivate staff by linking their personal goals to the company's aims.

USING EMPATHY

Empathy is sensitivity to the feelings of others. As a good manager, you must understand what makes staff tick in order to maintain their firm commitment. Devote time to finding links between staff capabilities and goals. Your efforts will be rewarded by results. Learn to foster political know-how. Be aware of who wields power in your organization, which sensitive toes to avoid, and who is likely to support or oppose a proposal.

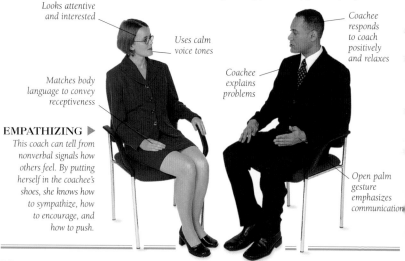

Looks attentive and interested

Uses calm voice tones

Matches body language to convey receptiveness

Coachee responds to coach positively and relaxes

Coachee explains problems

EMPATHIZING ▶
This coach can tell from nonverbal signals how others feel. By putting herself in the coachee's shoes, she knows how to sympathize, how to encourage, and how to push.

Open palm gesture emphasizes communication

INFLUENCING PEOPLE

People with influence have presence. This comes from their confidence in their strengths, their ability to manage crises, and their belief in their ideas. Show confidence and credibility in your demeanor. When confronted with conflict, seek out the other person's values and find ways of satisfying them with proposals. Fine-tune communication to suit the people you are influencing. If a colleague responds best to visual information, then influence them by using pictures or charts.

EXUDING CONFIDENCE ▶
Good managers listen to views different from their own. They hear employees' concerns and needs and take them into account before making any decisions of their own.

26 Be aware of nonverbal communication.

POINTS TO REMEMBER

- Good coaching requires high emotional intelligence.
- By demonstrating the qualities of motivation, empathy, sensitivity, and influence, you act as a role model to your staff.
- The more you encourage emotional intelligence in your staff, the easier it will be to coach them.
- When staff display emotional intelligence, praise them for it.

DEVELOPING EMOTIONAL INTELLIGENCE IN OTHERS

Coach your staff to improve their emotional intelligence by asking searching questions that prompt them to reflect on experience and learn from it. Give feedback that enables people to see themselves through others' eyes and discourage defensive thinking, while acknowledging the feelings of threat that underpin it. Ensure people take on responsibility for their own results and encourage them to consider the possible political sensitivities involved in their projects. Persuade staff to pursue challenging goals and provide the necessary support during difficult times.

▼ COACHING TACTICS
Question the coachee about past experiences and ask what can be learned from them. Challenge narrow thinking, and praise good work and performance to bolster the coachee's self-esteem.

| Question | ▶ | Challenge | ▶ | Praise |

DEVELOPING COACHING RELATIONSHIPS

Autonomy, initiative, decisiveness, and a sense of ownership for one's work are essential for both parties in a professional relationship. Encourage and develop these qualities in your staff to make them more receptive to a coaching approach.

27 Go out of your way to praise the achievements of your staff.

CULTURAL DIFFERENCES

Collaborative, participative attitudes to employee-manager working relations are fast gaining ground in both the US and the UK. In Japan, where the team is more important than the individual, participation is taken for granted within an overall structure of formal control.

ENCOURAGING AUTONOMY

Managers surrounded by independent staff will have more time to manage. Once managers have defined job responsibilities and reporting limits, then staff should be trusted to get on with the job in the best way they know how. Coaching is there to provide staff with a means of discussing pitfalls and brainstorming new ideas – not as a summons for orders and instructions. Let your staff learn to make their own decisions. Encourage autonomy by allowing your staff to learn from their mistakes and be ready to work with them to think through and build on what they learn.

ACHIEVING A GOOD COACHING RELATIONSHIP

A PRODUCTIVE RELATIONSHIP
A good coaching relationship is achieved by a combination of autonomy, shared responsibility, and the fostering of new skills.

● AUTONOMY
Coachee decides on the best options and relies on the coach for support when necessary.

● RESPONSIBILITY
Coach encourages the coachee to make decisions with a two-way coaching style.

● FOSTERING LEARNING
Coachee develops new skills with the support of the coach and sets new standards.

TREATING EMPLOYEES AS PARTNERS

Treating employees as partners fosters commitment and enterprise rather than compliance. Coaching is integral to this belief and places high emphasis on trust in the potential of individuals. Motivate employees by showing them that they have a valuable contribution to make.

Coach shows interest and respect for employee's views

Employee is confident about sharing ideas

SHARING IDEAS ▶
Encourage your team members to share their ideas on the best way to achieve your organization's goals.

QUESTIONS TO ASK YOURSELF

Q Am I letting fear stop me from delegating responsibility?

Q Do my staff each have a current project they can learn from?

Q Am I supportive of the ambitions of my staff?

Q Which members of my team are ready to step up a level?

Q Can I hand over a project to an able team member?

28 Set up progress reports for high risk projects and encourage the views of staff.

FOSTERING CONTINUOUS DEVELOPMENT

By asking "What can we learn from that?" or "What do we have to do next time to get a better result?," teams can come up with creative solutions that make the organization more efficient in the long run. Create a culture of opportunity in your team by continually setting new standards of excellence and using mistakes as springboards for new achievements. Keep looking for opportunities for your team to learn new skills, acquire new challenges, and expand their capabilities.

DO'S AND DON'TS

✔ Do let staff find their own best way to do the job.

✔ Do give people as much responsibility as they can handle.

✔ Do use the phrase "How can we..?," not "Why did you...?"

✘ Don't stifle effort and initiative with rules and regulations.

✘ Don't encourage staff to see you as the fount of all wisdom.

✘ Don't coach people beyond their limits of competence.

INITIATING COACHING

The first steps in a coaching cycle lay the foundations for its likely success. Be clear about when to start coaching, and how to structure and follow up a session.

PREPARING FOR A SESSION

Coaching can be spontaneous or formal. It can be given on a one-time basis or can work long-term over many sessions. It may be requested by the coachee, or called for by the coach. Whatever the situation, always clarify the purpose of a session.

29 Be clear about what you will work on during the session.

30 Mentally rehearse planned coaching sessions, but always be ready to adapt your approach.

NOTICING OPPORTUNITIES

Having ensured that the right conditions for coaching are in place – good coaching relationships, developmental opportunities, and motivated team members – look out for opportunities to offer coaching. An employee may approach you to discuss the possibility of promotion, and, in a coaching session, you can work together to identify paths to career development. Or, you may decide to call a coaching session when you notice an employee is having problems on a project. Always be ready to implement coaching when you see an appropriate moment, or when staff request it.

CLARIFYING NEEDS

Once a coaching opportunity has been noticed, it is important for both parties to be clear about what they are doing and how, where, and when coaching is going to work. If a member of your staff raises an issue that you feel may be resolved by coaching, ask if they would like some time with you to explore the issue. If you have noticed a performance problem that needs attention, then make it clear that you want to collaborate on finding a way to resolve it. In either case, be sure to state the benefits of a session and be clear about what you will work on.

POINTS TO REMEMBER

- Coaching off site can encourage a more open discussion.
- A coaching session should be uninterrupted.
- It is not necessary to say that you are going to "do coaching."

31 Agree on where and when you are going to meet.

ARRANGING A COACHING SESSION

LOCATION

MEETING ROOM
A private office enables the discussion to be confidential and uninterrupted.

OFF SITE
An informal, neutral location lends a more relaxed, less guarded air to the discussion.

PLANNED SESSION

- **AGREE ON TIMING**
Negotiate a time to meet and a length of session that suits both parties.

- **ALLOW SUFFICIENT TIME**
Overestimate the time required for the meeting and make allowances for the unexpected.

- **BOOK AHEAD**
Book two meetings in advance to ensure continuity, because people's calendars fill quickly.

- **MEET REGULARLY**
To make the best of time limitations, hold short coaching meetings on a regular basis.

SPONTANEOUS SESSION

- **BE FLEXIBLE**
Turn a question or complaint into an opportunity for spontaneous coaching.

- **BE CLEAR**
Make clear how much time you have at the outset of a session.

- **BE CONSIDERATE**
Ask the coachee how much time they have, in case they are worried about other commitments.

- **REVIEW**
Book a time and place for the next meeting, for feedback and further action.

STARTING A SESSION

Having prepared for coaching, you may want to hold a single session or you may decide to use the first session to initiate the coaching cycle. Whether coaching is initiated by you or by the coachee, outline what you aim to achieve in the session.

32 Start sessions positively and treat the coachee as an equal.

33 Divert calls to avoid unwanted interruptions.

MAKING A POSITIVE START

Your first remarks will set the tone for the rest of the session. Converse briefly about a positive, unrelated matter, such as a shared interest, to put the coachee at ease. Praise any achievements since you last met and allude specifically to work that has been well done. This will convey your positive interest and focus attention on performance. Agree on the length of the session so that you can set your sights on a realistic amount of ground to cover.

STARTING OUT ON THE RIGHT NOTE ▼
This coach warmly greets the coachee. His positive body language immediately puts the coachee at his ease.

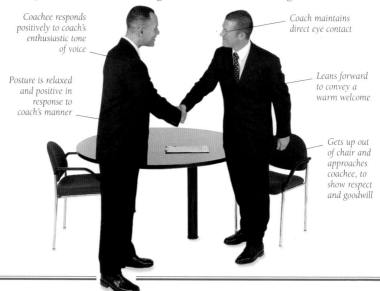

Coachee responds positively to coach's enthusiastic tone of voice

Posture is relaxed and positive in response to coach's manner

Coach maintains direct eye contact

Leans forward to convey a warm welcome

Gets up out of chair and approaches coachee, to show respect and goodwill

OUTLINING THE ISSUES

You may have called the session to focus on career development or to introduce a new procedure. In this case, outline the rationale for your interest. If you have called the coaching session to discuss a performance issue, then explain the problem. If the coachee agrees that the problem exists, then move on. If necessary, explain the consequences (to the coachee and the business) if the problem continues.

34 Emphasize your intent to support the coachee in solving issues.

THINGS TO DO

1. Acknowledge concerns and build a positive rapport.
2. Listen to comments and offer help in resolving outstanding issues.
3. Probe to find out what the coachee is aiming for.

WORKING WITH THE COACHEE'S AGENDA

If the session has been initiated by the coachee, restate your understanding of the reasons why the coachee has approached you and invite elaboration. Clarify points on which you are unclear, using simple questions such as "What do you mean by…?" If a developmental issue is on the agenda, find out what the coachee hopes to achieve and establish a clear basis for the session. Then begin coaching in a collaborative way.

ACHIEVING MUTUAL UNDERSTANDING

GIVING FEEDBACK

- **RELAX**
  You are offering an opinion, not imposing your interpretation as fact.

- **BE SPECIFIC**
  Call attention to the person's past behavior and its consequences.

- **INTERACT**
  Be prepared to listen, clarify, and expand. Be tactful and avoid casting blame.

- **SEEK AGREEMENT AND ACTION**
  Ask for the coachee's view and how he or she will act on your feedback.

RECEIVING FEEDBACK

- **BE OPEN**
  Feedback is crucial to development and learning, so listen attentively.

- **EVALUATE**
  Assess the validity of the feedback and the consequences of acting on it.

- **CLARIFY**
  Ask questions to clarify your understanding of the points made.

- **STATE YOUR VIEW**
  If you have a different view, offer it as another interpretation rather than as the "right" one.

SHAPING THE COACHING SESSION

Coaching is an organized way of generating ideas that raise individual performance. Use the GROW model to structure your work: define the Goals, explore present Reality, discuss Options, and agree on When an action will take place.

35 Well-defined, clear goals are at the heart of successful coaching.

GOALS
Define what is to be achieved

REALITY
Understand the situation

OPTIONS
Discuss choices available

WHEN
Agree on a course of action

SETTING GOALS

Good coaches ensure that both they and the individual know precisely what specific results are being sought. Many coaching sessions are based on little more than an exploration of what is to be achieved – and how, when, where, with whom, and why. Aim to form a coaching goal that is workable, operates within a realistic time frame, and is also achievable on the employee's present level of experience.

◀ **USING THE GROW MODEL**
You can start with any of the first three coaching steps, so long as they are all covered in one session and an agreement to a course of action is achieved.

CHECKING REALITY

Sometimes the coachee may begin a session by focusing on the reality of the situation. Be an excellent listener. In an atmosphere of attentiveness and support, employees are more likely to speak frankly about their problems and their personal limitations. Do not dwell on doubts, however. Encourage the coachee to move on as soon as possible to the consideration of options or goals.

36 Encourage staff to actively imagine doing better at something – they often go on to do so.

DISCOVERING OPTIONS

Coaching creates worthwhile opportunities by giving attention to the employee's strengths, to past accomplishments that can be adapted to the present, or by taking an imaginative look at new solutions. Some individuals may begin the session by wishing to discuss their good ideas and options with you. If so, praise their imaginative ideas, but be sure that you clarify what it is they will achieve (the goal) and how this will fit in with present conditions (reality).

DISCUSSING POSSIBLE OPTIONS ▶
Draw out ideas and solutions from the coachee. Opportunities can be discovered by going outside the individual's present frame of reference to other, more fruitful, perspectives.

37	Help the coachee look at a situation from a fresh angle.

38	Build on the coachee's past achievements.

DECIDING WHEN

Once goals have been defined, reality explored, and options established, it is up to the coachee to select the most inspiring or useful option and consider how it might be put into practice. Ensure that the session ends with a commitment to a specific action within a given time. This might be to gather information, confer with a colleague, or complete a task. Schedule the next coaching session so that the employee can report back on results. The coaching process can then begin again, using feedback as the basis for the next session's "reality."

DO'S AND DON'TS

✔ Do make rapport an important priority.

✔ Do be open, honest, patient, and persistent.

✔ Do consistently end coaching sessions by receiving commitment to an action.

✘ Don't close any options until the employee is ready to choose.

✘ Don't stop looking for opportunities to pin down achievable goals.

✘ Don't stop noticing nonverbal responses.

39	Arrange the next session before the meeting comes to an end.

DEFINING GOALS

Goal setting, the crux of coaching, is used to provide a structure for the coaching session itself and as a clear focus for resulting action. If time is limited, agree on a realistic goal for the session. Use the mnemonic SMART to focus on achievable results.

40 Use imagination to create, define, and explore an ideal outcome.

ANALYZING SITUATIONS

In order to establish definable goals, ask the coachee to imagine that he or she is working in an ideal way. Find out how this ideal differs from his or her current working patterns and procedures. Then ask what aspects of this "ideal" the coachee could realistically start to put into practice immediately.

AGREEING ON A MEETING GOAL

A goal for the meeting helps to focus coaching on the highest priorities. Agree on a coaching goal that can be achieved in the available time. Use it by asking yourself and the coachee if the meeting is progressing toward the goal. If not, work out how the session needs to change. If the goal is only partially addressed in the time, then schedule another session.

CREATING IDEAL GOALS

People often describe a means to an end rather than the end itself when they are asked to state their goals. The coachee may have an attractive goal in mind but rejects it because he or she sees too many problems in the way. Probe for what coachees really want. Uncover goals they will be motivated to achieve. Find out how things would look if there were no limits to what they could do. Once you have an ideal goal, find practical ways of achieving it.

▼ **IDENTIFYING IDEALS**
In this case, the coach acted as a catalyst and helped the manager recognize the real root of the problem, which she had previously overlooked.

CASE STUDY
In a coaching session between a sales director and a sales manager, the initial goal identified by the sales manager was to improve her forward planning. However, in reality, her ability to do this was hampered by many demands on her time. The coach asked her to imagine an ideal working environment. By looking at the problem from a different perspective, the big picture began to emerge.

In fact, the sales manager wanted a greater sense of control, rather than feeling she was reacting to others' demands. She wanted a better balance between her life at work and at home. After the coaching session, the manager made agreements with her sales director about her priorities and work schedules. She worked at home for one day each week on projects, and the result was an improvement in her planning.

Setting Specific Goals

The ideal aim becomes the specific goal to work toward. Use the mnemonic SMART as a tool for turning an ideal coaching goal into a specific goal. The "S" of SMART stands for Specific: you must precisely define the aim. "M" stands for Measurement: identify standards with which to assess achievement. "A" stands for Achievable: ensure the coachee has the resources needed to accomplish the goal. "R" stands for Relevant: check that the goal is worthwhile for the coachee. "T" is for Timed, representing the completion date.

41 Ask the coachee to imagine what they will see, hear, and feel when they have achieved a goal.

Reach the Moon

President John. F. Kennedy's speech to Congress on May 25, 1961, is a superb example of a goal that combines the ideal with SMART. In it, he stated his belief that the US should work toward the goal of landing a man on the Moon within 10 years. He emphasized the magnitude of the project for mankind, and he outlined specifically what would need to be done to achieve the goal. In a sense, the entire nation would be working together to put one man on the Moon.

Questions to Elicit SMART Goals

Elements of SMART	Useful Questions
Specific Ensure everyone knows the aim.	● What will you be doing when you have achieved the goal? ● What do you want to do next?
Measured Define standards to work toward.	● How will you measure the achievement of the goal? ● What will you feel when the goal is reached?
Achievable Ensure that the goal is realistic.	● What might hinder you as you progress toward the goal? ● What resources can you call upon?
Relevant Make sure the goal is worthwhile.	● What do you, and others, get out of this? ● Have other parties involved agreed to it?
Timed Agree on a time frame.	● When will you achieve the goal? ● What will be your first step?

CHECKING REALITY

B*efore looking at potential ways forward, it is vital to compare the coachee's present skill level with the desired one. This comparison may be obscured by worries and concerns. Listen attentively to these and be ready to assess present performance levels.*

42 Keep things clear and simple by asking direct questions.

43 Always keep the purpose of the session in mind.

44 Let staff vent their true feelings and clear the air.

DEALING WITH CONCERNS

Some employees may view coaching as a chance to offload complaints rather than work on their performance. Let the coachee feel heard without allowing the session to be deflected from the coaching aim. Distinguish between complaints about matters that are beyond the coachee's control and concerns that they can do something about. Ask if they have already explored a solution.

▼ **LISTENING WITH CARE**
In this coaching session, the coach draws out the coachee's worries to get to the root of the problem. He watches the coachee's body language to gain valuable insights into the issue.

Coach adopts sympathetic tone of voice

Direct gaze shows attention and interest

Coachee's averted gaze denotes uncertainty

Relaxed posture invites trust

Defensive posture shows lack of confidence

Open body language conveys willingness to help

Hand gesture shows eagerness to communicate

POINTS TO REMEMBER

- The flow of ideas should be maintained during the session.
- It is important to understand what the speaker is saying from his or her perspective.
- Show interest with nonverbal communication and use phrases such as "I see" and "Mm-hm" to signal understanding.
- You can subtly control the conversation by an exhalation of breath or a change of expression.

CONTROLLING THE FLOW

Listen to the coachee's responses to your questions. Avoid becoming overwhelmed with information. If the session starts to lose direction, politely stop the coachee and summarize what has been said. Ask a question that clarifies a point or leads on to considering a possible option. Alternatively, challenge what has been said and ask how it is relevant to the coachee's or team's goals. Use hand gestures to signal a pause for reflection or a slow-down in the flow of information, and ask the coachee where he or she thinks the session is going.

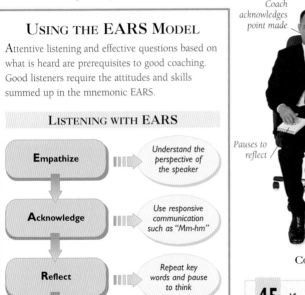

USING THE EARS MODEL

Attentive listening and effective questions based on what is heard are prerequisites to good coaching. Good listeners require the attitudes and skills summed up in the mnemonic EARS.

LISTENING WITH EARS

Empathize	▷	Understand the perspective of the speaker
Acknowledge	▷	Use responsive communication such as "Mm-hm"
Reflect	▷	Repeat key words and pause to think
Summarize	▷	Frequently summarize what has been said

Coach acknowledges point made

Leans back to denote a pause

Gestures to slow speaker down

Pauses to reflect

Retains open, positive body language

COACH

45 If you find yourself getting confused then say so, and ask for clarification.

RECOGNIZING NONVERBAL SIGNALS

People rely as much on the way things are said as on what is said. During a coaching session, take note of tones of voice, facial expressions, and hand gestures. Is the speaker coming across as active, positive, and focused? Or passive, confused, and self-divided? If the former, then press on with questions concerning options and goals. If the latter, then make time to explore the basis of the problem and be ready to lend more support. Listen to concerns that are barriers to achieving goals.

46 Understanding body language gives you insight.

47 Be aware that your expressions mirror your thoughts.

Restless gaze indicates thoughts are elsewhere

Folded arms form a barrier to communication

▲ **SHOWING PREOCCUPATION**
Avoidance of eye contact and fidgeting may indicate preoccupation with other matters. Ask the coachee if there is something on his or her mind.

Hunched shoulders are defensive

Frown denotes disagreement

▲ **SHOWING DISAGREEMENT**
A frown and hunched shoulders may reveal skepticism or even anger. Ask for the coachee's thoughts on what has just been said.

Averted eyes indicate evasiveness

Watching the time denotes restlessness

▲ **REVEALING DISINTEREST**
Restless movements, checking the time, and averted eyes could denote lack of interest. Ask the coachee how the session can be brought back on track.

Ear pulling indicates doubt

Faraway look shows uncertainty

▲ **INDICATING UNCERTAINTY**
When hands touch the face, particularly the ears, this can demonstrate uncertainty or doubt. Ask if there is a matter that the coachee needs to discuss.

ASSESSING WITH SCALES

Scales are a simple way of establishing present skill level and comparing it to the desired one. By asking the coachee for their thoughts on their own performance, it is possible to get to the roots of potential problems and establish what has to happen for performance to be improved. Ask the speaker to rate their assessments on a scale of 0–10 (with 10 representing the highest point on the scale). Then ask: "What has to happen for you to move up another point on this scale?" Self-ratings can be applied to confidence or motivation levels, and past performance.

Ask the coachee "What will you be doing when you reach 9 on the scale?"

Ask "What needs to happen before you can rate at 8 or 9 for motivation?"

Ask "What would have to happen for your confidence level to go up to 7?"

Ask "What can be done on a future project, for your rating to go up to 9?"

Assessing Performance

What rating would you give yourself for the way you handled that meeting?
1 2 3 4 5 6 7 (8) 9 1 0

How motivated are you to complete this?
1 2 3 4 5 6 (7) 8 9 1 0

Are you confident that you have the necessary skills to complete this project satisfactorily?
1 2 3 4 (5) 6 7 8 9 1 0

How confident are you that you can finish this project on time?
1 2 3 4 5 (6) 7 8 9 1 0

How did you rate your performance on the project you have just completed?
1 2 3 4 5 6 7 (8) 9 1 0

▲ MOVING UP THE SCALE
By establishing a present level of skill, confidence, or motivation, the coach can help identify a route to improvement.

---

48 Use a scale to help staff assess their present skill levels, and to assess their commitment to a goal.

CODE OF CONFIDENTIALITY

The golden rule of coaching is that everything that is said between a coach and coachee is confidential. You may hear of things that call for action outside the coaching session. If so, make it clear that you intend to preserve the anonymity of the coachee. If this is impossible, then ask for permission to share the information with those who need to know. However, aim to achieve openness in your team.

QUESTIONS TO ASK THE COACHEE

Q What do you notice is unusual about...?

Q What is another way of looking at this problem?

Q Can I check that I have got this right...?

Q How is this relevant to what we have been saying so far?

Q What has to happen for us to solve this?

Q Is there anything important that we've missed?

Q What will you have to do to move up the scale?

LOOKING FOR OPTIONS

Present strengths, past successes, and the difference between effective and less effective performance, all represent a gold mine of resources to be used in the service of achieving desired goals. Ask questions that encourage creative answers.

49 Make it known that you have high expectations of success.

THINGS TO DO

1. Find out what the coachee is good at and how these strengths can be utilized.
2. Match these strengths to the goal aimed for.
3. Find out about the coachee's past successes.
4. Use successful past actions to solve present problems.
5. Identify specific tasks that employ the coachee's skills.

EXPLOITING STRENGTHS

Mobilize people's talents and capabilities in the search for new ways to achieve goals. If you ask people what they like or enjoy, very often they will tell you what they are good at. When they reply, notice what excites or enthuses them. This is a good clue to what their strengths and preferences are. Chatting about work or nonwork matters during the session can also reveal people's abilities, as they tend to talk naturally about what they are enjoying at the moment or what interests them. Once you have identified a strength, determine how this particular skill can be used to good effect in the future. Use your creativity to link strengths to future tasks or projects.

CASE STUDY

A manager was made chief executive of a subsidiary in Europe. Socializing with customers was key to success in the designated country. Unfortunately, the manager considered himself to be socially inept, scoring himself 0 out of 10 for social confidence and skill with senior customers. Working with an external coach, he identified personal strengths he could employ in such social situations. These were a love of sports, strategic thinking, and project management. His coach encouraged him to make detailed plans to entertain customers at major sporting events. He decided who he would take with him from his own organization to help with conversation and how he would prepare himself prior to meeting senior customers. Through coaching, he was able to tackle his new role with confidence.

◀ **BUILDING ON STRENGTHS**
Through the help of a coach, this manager was able to identify what he was naturally good at and what he found difficult. He was able to adapt his working situation to build on his strengths and plan around his weaknesses.

NOTICING DIFFERENCES

Raise awareness in a coachee of the difference between effective and ineffective performance. In this way, the coachee can learn to recognize, and put into action, behavior appropriate for a particular situation. If, for example, the coachee is having a problem handling a "difficult" colleague, then ask the coachee to remember a time when the colleague was handled well. Eventually, the coachee will learn to be reflective about personal performance without your help.

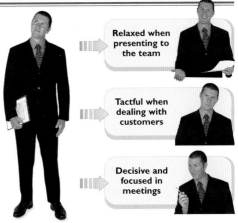

Relaxed when presenting to the team

Tactful when dealing with customers

Decisive and focused in meetings

▲ **REFLECTING ON PAST PERFORMANCE**
Encourage your coachees to actively recall a past situation where they performed well. Ask them to imagine doing the same thing in the future in a situation where that particular quality is called for.

50 Draw out the difference between present experience of a problem and a past success.

FINDING EXCEPTIONS

An exception is an instance in a person's past when a similarly challenging goal was achieved. To find such exceptions, ask when, in the past, the coachee has risen to a similar challenge. Set up a scale of 0–10, with 10 as the ideal solution. Ask the coachee to rate the present situation on the scale. Then ask if, in the past, the person would have rated higher up the scale than now, and why this should be.

ASSUMING SUCCESS

Encouraging high expectations leads to better performance. Do this by choosing words that assume success. For instance: "As you walk into the meeting feeling confident, what will you be thinking?" or "When you have broached this difficulty with the customer, what difference will it make to how you feel?" These questions assume a successful and constructive outcome. People accept positive expectation and are likely to live up to it.

QUESTIONS TO ASK THE COACHEE

Q What has worked in this situation before?

Q What was different about a past success?

Q When you achieve the goal, how will you feel?

Q What would a person you admire do?

CREATING NEW PERSPECTIVES

In the search to perceive new possibilities, focus on, or "frame," a situation to look at an issue from a different viewpoint. Use as much creativity as you can to help individuals to develop frames that foster creativity and solve problems.

51 Look at problems from every angle in order to find possible solutions.

52 Always listen to opposing points of view.

FRAMING PERSPECTIVES

One way to think about perspectives is as a series of frames. Each time we adopt a particular point of view we frame the things around us so that we can categorize them, understand them, and respond to them. When listening to the coachee's opinions, always bear in mind that the description is created from one particular viewpoint. This is especially true when an individual is stuck with what seems like an irredeemable problem.

▼ CONSIDERING DIFFERENT VIEWS

A salesperson has a customer who has problems with a product. Her coach encourages her to consider the points of view of her colleagues before taking discussions with the customer further.

The manager focuses on how to improve the service

The salesperson focuses on the problem with the product. The coach encourages her to talk to her colleagues for their points of view

As a result of the salesperson's consultations with her colleagues, the team re-presents the issue in a constructive way to the customer

The sales team focuses on how to keep the customer happy

CREATING FRAMES

Creative people use frames to look at things from fresh angles. Leonardo da Vinci framed paint blots on the wall as landscapes, to get ideas for his drawings. Similarly, an advertising agent might frame a new toy from a child's point of view to note product features that can be emphasized in an advertisement. Develop frames by asking how things look from the point of view of an existing customer, in a year's time or five year's time, or from the point of view of two very different customers.

53 Use imaginative frames to get new ideas on a project.

DEFINING FRAMES

TYPE OF FRAME	DEFINITION
PROBLEM FRAME	When everything is seen as a problem.
LEARNING FRAME	When everything is seen as a learning opportunity.
DETAIL FRAME	When the focus is on one element of an issue.
BIG PICTURE FRAME	When the focus is on the whole issue.
PERSONAL FRAME	When you focus only on what is happening to you.
TEAM FRAME	When you notice how events affect the team.
CONFLICT FRAME	When the focus is on disagreement.
NEGOTIATION FRAME	When the focus is on resolving conflict.

FRAME SWITCHING

An issue can appear to be an insurmountable problem. Encourage your team to view issues through another "frame," so they can be seen instead as a challenging goal, or as part of a bigger picture. Here are some useful questions to encourage "frame switching":

Problem Frame to Learning Frame
66 *What can we do about that?* 99

Personal Frame to Team Frame
66 *What is best for the team?* 99

Detail Frame to Big Picture
66 *Can we step back from this for a moment?* 99

Conflict Frame to Negotiation Frame
66 *What do you think would motivate them?* 99

TAKING ACTION

The focus of a coaching session is to pinpoint issues and to plan a course of positive action made up of specific tasks. At the end of a session, gain agreement and commitment to an action plan, which can be reviewed and assessed at a later date.

54 Prepare for a challenging event with constructive mental rehearsal.

SETTING TASKS

The options uncovered during the session provide the basis for action. The tasks agreed upon must move the coachee nearer to the agreed upon goal. Choose tasks that match the coachee's competence and level of confidence. Agree on a task that extends the coachee, but not so far that there is an unacceptable chance of failure. Ensure that the tasks are within the coachee's scope and will help build on or develop new skills. In either case, you should be ready to support coachees as they learn from any mistakes they make while following through the action plan.

55 Agree on and set achievable tasks that stretch a coachee's talents.

EXAMPLES OF TYPICAL TASKS

TASK SET	AIM OF ACTION
REVIEW COMMITMENTS	The coachee needs to prioritize the most important issues.
MEET WITH DECISION-MAKER	The coachee aims to get approval on a new business approach.
DISCUSSION WITH THE TEAM	A new way of working can be found by assessing feedback with the team.
TAKE TIME OUT TO CONSIDER	The coachee needs to ensure that the project is on track.
MEET WITH COLLEAGUE	The coachee needs to implement a changed approach to a meeting.
MEET WITH CUSTOMER	The customer needs reassurance about the progress of a project.

GETTING AGREEMENT

When staff are involved in decisions, and agree to a task, they are more likely to feel a sense of ownership for it. Ensure agreement at this stage by summarizing the options discussed and asking which ones are most likely to be successful. Once a selection has been made, test your understanding in order to solidify agreement. For example, you could consolidate the agreement by saying: "Let me check that I understand so far. You have decided that when an unexpected assignment is handed to you, you will ask for time to think it over. Once you have considered the implications, you will take it on or not, consulting your manager as necessary."

56 Make your staff accountable for their results.

57 Be prepared to offer your own opinion, without imposing it.

Asks questions

Leans forward

SHOWING COMMITMENT

Unresponsive to questions

Turns away

SHOWING NONCOMMITMENT

ASSESSING COMMITMENT

When an ambitious action plan is discussed, commitment needs to be high, as it may require a significant change in behavior. If commitment is low, then other priorities are likely to override change. Assess commitment by asking questions that probe for enthusiasm. Watch carefully for nonverbal signs that indicate motivation. Increase commitment by asking how the coachee will feel when the job is done. Ask the coachee what can be done to resolve any doubts.

◀ **NOTING COMMITMENT**
When the coachee is replying to your questions, notice signs of commitment, such as an interested posture and definite answers. A wavering look and a slouching posture can both denote noncommitment.

OFFERING SUPPORT

As the coachee prepares to take action, offer support without undermining the coachee's sense of responsibility. Make it clear that you are available to be used as a sounding board to work out ideas or explore solutions to problems. In this way, you act as a catalyst, enabling change rather than directing it. Provide your support if your seniority is needed to influence other senior managers, or to gain the cooperation of other team members.

THINGS TO DO

1. Ask the coachee to identify issues or tasks for which he or she needs support.
2. Let the coachee know when you are going to be available to give support.
3. Make sure other team members are working toward the same goal, so that there are no conflicts.

COACHING TO SUCCEED ▼
As a coach, you should be supportive, act as a mediator of ideas, ensure there are no barriers to success, and, if necessary, mobilize the resources needed to achieve the goal.

| **Be supportive** | → | **Act as a catalyst** | → | **Use your influence** |

PLANNING ACTION

The tasks agreed on must be turned into a solid action plan that can be reviewed. Either work out the plan with the coachee during the coaching session, or agree that the coachee can develop a plan before the next coaching session. Set a review date and agree on the location for the next session. This gives a point in time to work toward so that the coachee knows that certain tasks have to be completed by this date. Once agreed on, the coachee needs to make notes on results achieved and further actions to be taken.

Course of action decided, and tasks set

Sales manager gives necessary support

Goal is outlined

SAMPLE ACTION PLAN ▶
This coaching plan was formed between a sales manager and his assistant to agree on how a customer complaint will be dealt with.

Plan is formed to deal with a customer complaint

Coaching Plan
Resolving a Complaint

Action:
Sales assistant to telephone the customer and ask for details of the wrong delivery. Organize meeting with Operations Manager.

Deadline for Action:
7th May.

Resources Required:
Sales Manager to look at discount policy and speak to Operations Manager before meeting.

Results Required:
Customer to send in receipt and Operations Manager to investigate problem and offer customer a discount.

Review:
On May 20th, in main meeting room.

Review date and location is set

Coach offers support and acts as a catalyst to overcome problems

Completion and review dates are agreed

Coachee has doubts

Solid action plan is determined

Ambitious action plan is discussed

Coach and coachee consider options

▲ **AGREEING ACTION**

In this example, the coach and coachee meet to form an action plan. The coachee has doubts about the plan, and the coach must work to keep the meeting on track.

Coach and coachee fail to reach agreement

MANAGING RISKS

Although you want to stretch the capabilities of your staff, you need to insure against failure. Any task with a high risk attached to it is one in which failure could damage the reputation of yourself, the coachee, or your organization. Manage risks by discussing the actions the coachee plans to implement. Then monitor the results and agree on reviews without undue interference. When the risk is low because staff are competent or the task is simple, ask them to act first and then report.

58 Show loyalty to your staff even if things go wrong, and help them identify lessons for the future.

QUESTIONS TO ASK THE COACHEE

Q What option do you think will work best?

Q How soon are you able to start working on this?

Q What will be your first step toward achieving your goal?

Q When will you take the action we have agreed on?

Q When can we meet to review your progress?

FOLLOWING UP

Coaching – like any learning process – is continual. Each coaching session leads to action, followed by either success or feedback on what must be done next time. Put in place follow-up procedures that initiate an upward spiral of achievement.

59 Ask your staff to tell you what they have learnt from recent projects.

60 Keep spaces in your calendar so you are able to give extra coaching if necessary.

FOLLOWING UP SESSIONS

Keep up the momentum of learning. Make links between the work completed in the current session and the agreed action plan, and then to follow-up sessions. Arrange the next meeting at the end of each session, and aim for this to coincide with the completion of the agreed action plan. Explain that this next meeting will begin with a briefing from the coachee about how the action plan has been carried out and what the results were.

MONITORING CHANGE

When arranging projects that consolidate new skills, ensure your staff feel confident about what they are to do. Smaller projects are favorable if the employee is inexperienced. Small successes lead to bigger wins, gathering momentum with each new achievement. The other thing you can offer as a coach in between sessions is support. Let your staff know that you are always on hand for consultations if they need them. Once you hear that goals have been achieved, acknowledge success and deliver praise.

▼ **ASSESSING DEVELOPMENT**
A key role of a manager is to develop staff's potential. By offering support, you are also in a position to assess progress.

Coach gives constructive feedback

RESETTING STRETCH GOALS

Momentum for existing changes will slow down as the employee becomes more experienced. Coaching requires that the coachee is continually being stretched, or challenged, in order to improve on past levels of performance. As you continue to coach, periodically reset employees' performance goals by asking them to come up with new challenges. If they do not have any ideas themselves concerning their next performance targets, then look out for new responsibilities to assign to them, and get ready to delegate.

REACHING FOR SUCCESS ▶

Encourage your staff to reach slightly beyond their perceived limits when reviewing their next goal. Ensure that each new goal represents a definite advance on the previous level of competence.

61 Encourage team members to coach each other.

62 Set an example by seeking coaching yourself.

COACHING VALUES ▼

Encourage staff to coach themselves and team members to coach each other, either formally or informally.

INSTILLING COACHING ATTITUDES

As a manager, your eventual aim as a coach is to build a coaching team. To do this requires that all members of the team are able to coach themselves, and each other. Advance this teaching process by explaining the four steps of coaching (GROW) and encouraging employees to use it whenever working problems and opportunities arise. Ask participants to prepare for team coaching sessions by defining goals, writing a brief description of the issues at stake, mentioning some options, and recommending a proposed course and date of action. In this way you will be encouraging your staff to be their own coaches.

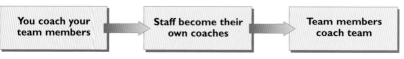

| You coach your team members | ▶ | Staff become their own coaches | ▶ | Team members coach team |

MAKING COACHING WORK

When coaching attitudes are introduced into traditional business environments, misunderstandings can arise. Overcome doubts with tact, persistence, and insight.

COACHING ATTITUDES

For the coaching approach to become an accepted working practice on your team, you should be seen as a good role model for coaching. Act on the beliefs, values, and attitudes that underpin the approach, and encourage your team to participate in them.

63 Discourage perfectionism – always seek to develop realism.

64 Treat achievements as stepping stones to future success.

65 Treat setbacks as lessons to be learned from, and then move on.

APPRECIATING SUCCESS

Coaching is based on appreciative inquiry. It actively assumes that successes are inevitable and looks for opportunities to acknowledge these when they occur. Coaches recognize success in teams that cope with adversity, in individuals who learn to master skills, and in organizations that adapt to change. This does not mean that all successes are to be rewarded, but that there is a focus on gains as opposed to losses. Gains represent actual and potential success and are there to be used in the future. Celebrate your team's achievements and find ways to use these in the future.

FOCUSING ON THE POSSIBLE

Problems are easy to find and magnify. The complex nature of many organizations, and the markets in which they operate, means that control over outcomes is often beyond the scope of managers. In practice, you have to make do with the possible rather than with the ideal. Be pragmatic rather than demanding. Be practical rather than perfectionist.

Solution focused: looks for options

Self-starting: shows strong motivation

Practical: focuses on the achievable

Responsible: sees job through to the end

Proactive: plans ahead

Takes initiative: makes decisions

▲ COACHING ATTITUDES
Coaching is an approach that develops good attitudes and a set of values in your staff. As you display these qualities yourself, your good example spreads to the rest of your team.

POINTS TO REMEMBER

- A good coach remains composed under pressure, focusing on what is in their power to change.
- When crises occur, you should lead by example and show staff you are helping to solve the issue.
- Everyone benefits when you influence the situation rather than blame others.
- Staff should be responsible for any mistakes they make.

TAKING OWNERSHIP

Ownership means taking responsibility for oneself and one's work. Managers who take ownership will accept that they are accountable for the work of everybody in the team, not just their own work. When the work of an individual team member is criticized, support the individual and be seen to be taking responsibility for corrections. To encourage responsibility in your team, delegate ownership for a task to an employee, within the limits of their present skills. Exercise a hands-off policy unless the employee asks you for help.

ACKNOWLEDGING VIEWS

The efforts of each individual team member are reliant on the efforts of all the other members. To this end, make room for a variety of specializations, ideas, and approaches within a team. A team can benefit from having, for example, a creative planner, a dynamic go-getter, and a reflective critic. Accepting personal differences between team members means ensuring that their voices are heard and their contributions appreciated. Encourage team members to share their ideas.

66 At meetings, stick to the agenda, while encouraging suggestions from all parties present.

DEALING WITH BARRIERS TO COACHING

Coaching is a modern approach to management, and it can raise fear or distrust in those unfamiliar with it. Deal with misconceptions about coaching by explaining its benefits and be ready to defuse misunderstandings.

67 Treat suspicion as a comment on the past, rather than on the present.

POINTS TO REMEMBER

- Openness can be built by encouraging employees to voice concerns.
- Coaching should develop at a pace the coachee is comfortable with.
- Differences of opinion should be worked through.
- If you practice what you preach, resentment can be avoided.

HANDLING MISTRUST

Coaching works only if there is a bond of trust between the parties involved. The coach must ensure that the employee is speaking openly and honestly. In turn, the coachee needs to feel sure of the coach's loyalty and willingness to understand. Suspicion can be based on a sense that the organization or its management are not practicing what is being preached. If so, be ready to give evidence that you and your organization are actively practicing coaching attitudes.

OVERCOMING RELUCTANCE

The most common reason for avoidance of coaching lies in misunderstanding. Check that your staff realize that coaching is designed to help them achieve success. Stress the benefits of coaching and its potential for gaining the coachee greater recognition within the organization. It is also important to check whether there is a need for coaching. Often, highly motivated and able employees may not require coaching for the work they are currently doing. In this case, ask the employee to list their longer-term career aims and make this the basis for agreed upon coaching goals.

68 Be ready to resolve past conflicts openly.

69 Ask how staff would like to be coached and adapt your approach.

DEALING WITH MISCONCEPTIONS

MISCONCEPTION	RESPONSE
"COACHING IS FOR STAFF WHO ARE FAILING IN THEIR WORK" Coaching is stigmatic and disciplinary. It is a form of retraining for people who are unable to do their job properly.	Coaching is for people who want to do better and meet new challenges. It helps people explore their potential beyond the work they are currently involved in.
"COACHING IS A FORM OF COUNSELING" Coaching is an excuse for people to offload problems or complaints, and discuss personal emotions.	Counseling is reactive. Coaching is the opposite. It is proactive, goal focused, and seeks to improve personal and organizational performance.
"COACHING IS A NEW MANAGEMENT FAD" Coaching has been introduced because other initiatives have failed.	Coaching has potential benefits for the employee, the team, and the manager. It is worth making it work, irrespective of people's past experiences.
"COACHING MEANS MORE WORK FOR LESS MONEY" Coaching will lead to an increased workload, without any rewards for staff.	When performing at their best, staff find work easier and more rewarding. Coaching can focus on those areas of work in which you would like to solve problems, simplify the issues, and streamline your efforts.

DO'S AND DON'TS

✔ Do practice what you preach.	✘ Don't lose patience – old habits die hard.
✔ Do look at problems from the individual's point of view.	✘ Don't wait for confusion to spread – deal with it at once.
✔ Do keep stressing the benefits of coaching.	✘ Don't coach if the time isn't right.
✔ Do remain calm in the face of opposition.	✘ Don't worry if progress is slow.

70 Show others that coaching works by outlining successful examples.

TROUBLESHOOTING

Despite your best efforts, coaching may not always work. Most of the pitfalls are common, however, and can be thoughtfully dealt with. If necessary, go back to basics, ask searching questions to find the root of the problem, and refocus priorities.

71 Be open to a dialogue with staff and take heed of their suggestions.

72 Introduce coaching gradually to staff with misgivings.

73 Always address causes rather than symptoms.

ADDRESSING MISGIVINGS

Some people are skeptical. They distrust the coach or doubt the benefits of coaching. Be open to a dialogue with staff and take heed of their suggestions. If the culture does not immediately support coaching, introduce it slowly. Ask questions rather than give answers, but do not overdo it. Be aware that there are occasions when people need straight answers, for example, a quick decision during the heat of a negotiation. As a manager, make decisions when needed, and coach people before and after the event.

FINDING THE CAUSE

In the long term, a coaching cycle that addresses causes rather than symptoms is more likely to succeed. For example, you could deal with a workload problem by relieving an employee of certain tasks. This could solve the immediate problem but not the long-term one. Reflect on the stages in the project where the problem could have arisen. The cause could be that the employee takes on too much work to please you, without considering the consequences.

Coach thinks through possible roots of problem

ASSESSING ROOTS OF PROBLEMS ▶
There may be a number of barriers to coaching. Search for the underlying roots to a problem, such as fear of change, dependency, or skepticism.

DEALING WITH BACKSLIDING

Problems can occur when the coachee does not have the know-how, commitment, or resources, including time, to do a job. Ensure that the necessary conditions exist for the goal to be achieved by equipping the coachee with the necessary skills. Focus their commitment by showing how the challenge will benefit the coachee personally. Check that there are no organizational barriers to the goals and that the coachee has the necessary resources and time to do the job.

POINTS TO REMEMBER

- You could brief your team and colleagues on a coaching method that has been successful in the past.
- Projects should be set off on the right note by using a coaching approach.
- Focus groups can be a useful way of avoiding pitfalls and determining how they can be overcome.

75 Break down challenges into smaller, less daunting steps.

ASSESSING CONDITIONS

SETTING GOALS
In order to achieve a goal, the coachee needs to know what to do, will want to do it, and will have the opportunity to do it.

KNOW-HOW
The coachee has been trained in the skills necessary for the job.

COMMITMENT
The coachee is motivated and understands how success will be personally rewarding.

OPPORTUNITY
The coachee has the necessary support and resources to do the job.

74 Support your staff by freeing up their time so that they are able to concentrate on achieving new goals.

OVERCOMING THE FEAR OF CHANGE

Being daunted by challenges, such as a change of role, or communication with the senior management team, can interfere with people's development. The new challenge may be daunting, and the employee may feel ready to give up when setbacks occur. Often, at the heart of the matter is a fear of failure and its consequences. You can lessen this by using a coaching approach: learning from mistakes rather than punishing errors. Another way of helping people take on new challenges is to find ways in which they can apply their present strengths by, for example, asking a good organizer to draw up a difficult work schedule for the team.

Overcoming Dependency

If your style in the past has been to give answers to your staff rather than to coach them, or if you have inherited a team from such a manager, then team members may habitually look to you to solve their problems. Deal with this by clarifying expectations. Agree on the kinds of issues you are prepared to discuss and how you expect these issues to be presented. Gradually, ask staff to outline their ideas for solutions so that you can discuss them. Ask them what they have already thought of and what other solutions exist.

76 Encourage staff to use their own initiative.

77 Learn to notice signs of over-dependency.

Recognizing Signs of Dependency

Sign	Symptom
No Thought	Staff nearly always ask you for the answers rather than working through a problem and coming up with a solution themselves.
No Confidence	People have a tendency to ask you to do things for them, rather than making decisions and taking concerted action.
No Foresight	Problems and opportunities are missed through lack of foresight or an inability to see the whole picture.
No Initiative	Staff rely on you to get things going rather than risk making mistakes and failing in the task themselves.

Do's and Don'ts

78 Show your staff that you trust and believe in their capabilities.

✔ Do watch out for signs that staff are getting too dependent on you.

✔ Do build confidence by showing that you expect staff to do well.

✘ Don't allow your staff to feel inadequate if they are unable to solve an issue alone.

✘ Don't change your style of management too abruptly.

Coachee is responsible for market research

Team is in charge of producing marketing plan

COACHEE

TEAM

DEPARTMENT

ORGANIZATION

Department is responsible for coordinating plan with manufacturing and sales

Organization aims to achieve new profit and revenue targets

◄ **TAKING AN OVERVIEW**
As a coach, help show your coachees how their roles and goals fit with those of their team, department, and organization. In this way, the coachees can learn to see the value of their contribution to the whole.

FOCUSING ON PRIORITIES

When coaching is not achieving its aim, it is important to listen to employees' problems and focus on priorities. When you talk about the actions people have taken to achieve a goal, talk around the subject and find out what enthuses them. Realign coaching goals with what you observe to be the most important priorities for your staff. Motivate your staff by showing them how their priorities align with the organization's interests, and by explaining how their work directly affects results. This leads to self-motivated staff.

**RECOGNIZING ►
STRENGTHS**

In this case study, the coach was able to build a coachee's confidence. By drawing on the coachee's existing strengths, he showed how these could be used in situations that seemed new or challenging.

CASE STUDY

A manager asked a coach for help in putting complex information given in meetings into logical order. The coach gave advice about note taking, mind mapping, and questioning techniques. However, the coach found that the manager already knew these techniques. The breakthrough in the coaching session came when the coach asked if there were times in the past when the manager had converted complex information from a meeting into logical notes. The manager acknowledged she had been able to do this in past meetings when her knowledge of the subject had given her mental pegs on which to hang the information. The coach subsequently focused on how the manager could do research before meetings so that she had mental pegs in mind and could approach note taking with new confidence.

DEALING WITH ORGANIZATIONAL BARRIERS

Barriers typically occur as organizations move from a traditional, directive management style to a coaching approach. Deal with these barriers by recognizing old attitudes and working to overcome them through education, example, and persistence.

79 Get the support of colleagues who also favor a coaching approach.

80 Encourage your staff to be more autonomous.

LEARNING TO LET GO ▼
Coaching can become impossible if you are doing the work of others as well as your own. Coach yourself to be disciplined about delegating tasks.

DEALING WITH OVERLOAD

Managers may be overloaded with responsibilities for a variety of reasons. You may be overloaded with work because you are carrying your employees' responsibilities. This may reflect the old attitude that managers are the only people who know how the job should be done. If so, deal with this gradually by encouraging your employees to make decisions without relying on you. Coach your employees to think through their own options

Manager tries to concentrate on a coaching plan

Manager does tasks left undone by team

Administrative tasks interrupt manager's day

MANAGING YOUR TIME

Coaching can take time in the short term, but it is a worthwhile investment of your hours. Coach your team to assume the responsibility for solving problems, while you get on with the job of managing. Prioritize important items and cut down on inefficient demands on your time. Coach yourself to do this by setting a goal of increasing the time available to you, analyzing your present workload, and generating options for reducing it.

81 Focus on long-term development rather than fire-fighting problems for short-term benefit.

QUESTIONS TO ASK YOURSELF

Q Does senior management adopt a coaching approach?

Q Does my senior manager support team development?

Q Does my team feel the organization supports its initiatives?

Q Do I set projects off on the right note by consistently using a coaching approach?

DEALING WITH INERTIA

For the coaching approach to become widely adopted it must be supported by all levels of management, as well as by the teams and employees involved. If it is not, then employees may become discouraged if they feel that their initiatives and improved performance are not achieving recognition from the organization. Old attitudes die hard, and it may take time before the coaching philosophy takes root. Deal with inertia by becoming an active agent for change.

OVERCOMING IGNORANCE

Talk to other managers about what you are trying to achieve with coaching. Give seminars on the coaching approach, explaining how it can influence the organization. Ask senior managers to hold briefings emphasizing the organization's support for coaching. Be ready to enter into a dialogue with critics by anticipating their objections and linking the benefits of coaching to their personal values. Show how coaching can free up management time once team members learn to become more independent.

▼ **INITIATING CHANGE**
Educate people in your organization and enlist their support by explaining how the coaching approach works and how it differs from other approaches to management.

REFINING COACHING

Be prepared to use coaching in a variety of situations. Coach your team, your external staff, and your colleagues to adopt coaching values, and delegate so you have time to manage and lead.

TEAM COACHING

The coaching process can be of equal value in coaching teams. Use the GROW model and adapt your coaching style by ensuring that teams share in the work of defining goals, generating options, and assuming responsibility for tasks.

82 Check that each team member is committed to the team's goal.

▲ **WORKING AS A TEAM**
Ask your team to work together to create inspirational goals. By asking them to imagine a desired future, the team can then work on turning an ideal into a goal.

AGREEING ON GOALS

It is essential that a team agree on shared goals in order to achieve optimum performance. Clarify goals at the start of a project, or when an operational problem needs to be solved. At a coaching session, ask team members to summarize their understanding of present goals or to suggest new goals. Encourage your team to come up with creative ideas, then use ideal goal questions. Take the shared ideas and make them work by turning them into SMART goals.

ASSESSING REALITY

Each person's view of reality depends on his or her perspective. Ensure these different views are aired. During the session, set up a scale to represent the extremes of performance at, for example, project start and finish. Ask the team members to give their present assessment ratings privately. Then, ask them to declare their ratings. Explore the reasons for differences of opinion.

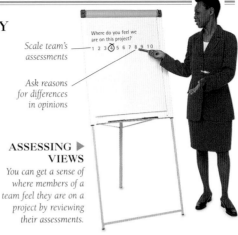

Where do you feel we are on this project?
1 2 3 ④ 5 6 7 8 9 10

Scale team's assessments

Ask reasons for differences in opinions

▶ **ASSESSING VIEWS**
You can get a sense of where members of a team feel they are on a project by reviewing their assessments.

83 Explore differences of opinion so that team members learn to see each other's viewpoints.

EXPLORING OPTIONS

The gap between goals and reality now needs to be closed. Searching for exceptions and brainstorming are two ways that can help. To find exceptions, the team can discuss successful projects of the past. The lessons can then be applied to the present project. Encourage the team to brainstorm ideas and suspend criticism. Then evaluate the ideas against an agreed upon set of criteria to select the most promising for action.

DECIDING WHEN

In the coaching session, make a point of taking a break between the options and action phase of GROW. A coffee break can be an ideal way to punctuate a session and make an action plan memorably stand out against the background of a meeting. On resumption of the session, identify the specific tasks to be done. Be sure that accountability for each task is assigned clearly and agree on the completion dates. Check that everyone agrees to the plan. If you see signs of uncertainty, ask questions to find out the reasons behind it.

84 Clearly assign specific tasks to individuals.

85 Resolve issues at the early stage of an action plan.

COACHING LONG DISTANCE

Managers with team members who work in the field, or at some distance from the office, may communicate mainly by phone or email. Make sure face-to-face meetings are utilized to maximum effect and that responsibilities are clear-cut.

86 Maintain contact with field staff at the same time each week.

ORGANIZING LONG-DISTANCE COACHING

The coaching process can be completed with any combination of telephone coaching, email correspondence, video conferencing, and face-to-face meetings. Conduct the first session in person, so that a mutually agreeable format for coaching can be discussed. Further communications may be used to provide progress reports, feedback on results, and discussions on how actions could be amended. However, performance issues are best dealt with face-to-face.

▼ OUTLINING METHODS
Meet your field staff to discuss the coaching cycle. Explain that you will use face-to-face sessions for big issues, telephone calls for reviews, and emails for progress checking.

Coach outlines coaching cycle

Salesman agrees to method of coaching

87 Always keep communications interruption-free.

88 Provide regular briefings on issues to field staff.

DO'S AND DON'TS

✔ Do make sure you coach face-to-face at regular intervals.

✔ Do consider video conferencing facilities if available.

✔ Do be punctual for telephone meetings.

✘ Don't let telephone calls lose the point.

✘ Don't forget to follow up telephone calls with written summaries.

✘ Don't address complex coaching issues by email.

REVIEWING BY TELEPHONE

If the first progress report is to take place by telephone, plan the call to last around 15–20 minutes. Start by restating the goals and agreed upon actions, and ask for a brief summary of results. If things are going well and further coaching is not required at this point, then the telephone call can be rescheduled for a later time. If further coaching is required then begin by asking the coachee how they would like to use the available time in relation to the goal.

Uses questions to guide coachee

Updates coaching notes

▲ **COACHING BY PHONE**
Keep telephone coaching direct and to the point. Use simple questions, reminders, and suggestions to keep staff on track.

88 Use emails for suggestions or reminders.

89 Hold regular social events for all of your team.

E-COACHING

An effective means of virtual communication, emails are widely used by professional coaches. However, they should never be used as substitutes for personal coaching. Instead, they should be employed strictly as a follow-up to a personal coaching session. Email etiquette dictates that messages should be brief, condensed, and informal. Avoid long-winded messages and defer complex matters for personal communication.

CHECKING PROGRESS THROUGH EMAILS

When following up via emails, avoid messages that focus on problems. Use well-defined, simple, and constructive questions about goals. Keep communication short, simple, and direct. You are then more likely to receive quick and direct responses.

66 *Where are you with that project?* 99

66 *Have you discovered a better way to reduce costs?* 99

66 *The managing director is really excited by our ideas. Do you have any new ones for her?* 99

66 *I've heard that the project office has some experience with that client. Have you spoken to them recently?* 99

COACHING AND APPRAISING

Appraising can mean an informal evaluation by you of an individual's work or a more formal review process. Use coaching to enhance the appraisal process by identifying achievements and making sure new performance targets are realistic.

91 Give constructive and supportive feedback on past performances.

92 Praise staff achievements and link them to the prospect of future success.

HOLDING REVIEWS

Your organization may have a performance review process by which employees' past performance is evaluated and new goals set for the future. Apply a coaching approach to the review process. Look for opportunities to praise an employee's achievements and link them to the prospect of achievements to come. If it is necessary to discuss failures, invite the employee to discuss what happened, and what options are available for corrective action.

DEVELOPING EMPLOYEES

Within the appraisal interview, use open-ended questions to explore your employee's needs and aspirations. Ask about the next step needed to take the employee up to his or her desired standard of work. Coaching is a complementary process to the development of skills. When carrying out the appraisal, identify the skills required to achieve the agreed upon goals and set up training opportunities if necessary. This may be on-the-job or out-of-house training. Develop a plan through which employees can gradually introduce their newly acquired skills to specific projects.

Compare recent performance against past objectives

Ask about learning experiences and give feedback and praise

Identify and prioritize development options

Agree on new objectives and when they are to be achieved

Specify actions to be taken and devise schedule

REVIEWING AS A FORM OF COACHING ▶
Integrate coaching values and techniques into the review session by defining goals, assessing reality, discussing options, and agreeing on a schedule for when actions will be carried out.

LINKING TO REWARDS

Coaching is built on the premise that individuals are capable of using their abilities to become more successful than they are now. Bear in mind that a good result needs to be encouraged by linking it to rewards. These need not be material. Some of the most worthwhile rewards include praise, recognition, awards, and visible respect. Material rewards can range from company benefits to promotions, and salary increases. Reward each completion of a coaching performance target by a public recognition of the individual's achievement.

CULTURAL DIFFERENCES

Americans celebrate and praise success with great enthusiasm. In contrast, the British tend to mark success with a quiet, appreciative word. Formal recognition in German organizations may be followed up by more enthusiastic comment outside the work environment.

SETTING TARGETS AFTER A REVIEW ▼

Here is an example of a review carried out between a credit control supervisor and his manager, which resulted in a single developmental goal plan supported by training and coaching.

93 Achievements that are rewarded tend to be repeated.

Clear notes are used as a basis for the next review

A Coaching-Based Review

Last Period's Objectives:
Create new credit control system

Examples of achievements:
Developed new procedures. Learned to supervise new employees.

Employee's self-rating:
7. Would like to expand customer liaison.

Manager's Comments:
8. Kevin's results exceed expectation.

Next Period's Objectives:
Reduce average credit period to 40 days.

Employee's comments: Need to focus on problem spotting.

General Comments:
Coaching will establish ways in which Kevin's existing expertise can be applied.

Achievements are recorded

Goal is established

Employee assesses own performance

New targets are identified

Agreed upon plan is put in writing after review

Development Plan

Long-Term Objectives:
To increase customer-liaison role.

Immediate objectives:
To increase response rate with customers delaying settlement.

Competencies required:
Effective liaison skills

Training needs (if any):
2-day customer relations course.

Actions Agreed:
Take course within next three months and use follow-up coaching to implement new skills.

Review Date Agreed:
Date set for review of results.

A timeline is agreed on

Coach recognizes coachee's natural flair with customers

COACHING THROUGH DELEGATION

Coaching and delegation are complementary. As the continual learning cycle moves upward, team members become ready to assume responsibility for more complex tasks. You are then in a position to delegate, set new targets, and lead.

94 Raise your expectations and ask people to live up to them.

DELEGATING PROJECTS

Identify priorities and capabilities of coachee

⬇

Ensure that the delegated work represents more responsibility

⬇

Brief employee on what is to be achieved

⬇

Ask for ideas and show confidence and trust

⬇

Be available to offer support if necessary

⬇

Arrange for periodic reports on progress

PREPARING TO DELEGATE

Coaching requires the identification of ever-new performance targets for the next cycle of achievement. Remember that the latent talents to achieve new targets probably already exist within your team. Coach people in order to draw out these talents. As you notice that an employee starts to attain the necessary level of competence, get ready to delegate some of your own work. When coaching, bear in mind that the delegated work should represent an opportunity for genuine advancement in terms of increased skill and responsibility. Above all, empower your staff by letting them see your increasing confidence in them and by giving them opportunities to do things their way rather than yours. Use coaching to brief team members thoroughly, asking for ideas and then leaving them to get on with it under their own initiative.

95 Resolve any doubts by offering support and explaining how difficulties can be overcome.

DELEGATING PROJECTS

Let the team member know that they are progressing well and that you are ready to delegate an important project. Be sure to praise the employee's past performance. Set the agenda for the coaching session by introducing the project. Seek agreement from the coachee that they are ready for new responsibility and ensure that they are committed to the new venture.

Coachee expresses enthusiasm and interest

Coachee takes notes

Coach tells coachee she is ready for more responsibility

Project is presented and explained

96 Delegate work before it overwhelms you.

97 Allow people to learn from their own mistakes.

POINTS TO REMEMBER

● People remember more from their mistakes than from their successes.

● People have hidden talents that emerge when they are challenged.

● Staff blossom when they are trusted with jobs they do well.

▲ **HANDING OVER RESPONSIBILITY**
When you hand over a project, explain the background and specify the deadlines, available resources, and levels of authority in place. Make it clear what the employee is to achieve before considering the possible options for achieving it.

OFFERING SUPPORT

Coaches position themselves as supporters rather than authority figures. Offer support to the team members to whom you delegate. Make it clear that you are available for further brief or extended coaching sessions in relation to the delegated task. Avoid interference and do not give advice unless it is asked for. Exercise a "hands-off" policy once action plans have been agreed upon and leave employees to get on with things in their own way. Refrain from interfering in order to "save time" on the project and let delegates learn from their own mistakes. If you are called upon to help, ask the delegate to think through the problem prior to the coaching session and be ready to talk through their options with you.

EMPOWERING EMPLOYEES

Let employees know that they are entrusted with carrying out the work in the way they think best, within the parameters set for the job. Be aware that their approach may differ radically from yours. Work through any questions or doubts, and make suggestions that are designed to enhance options rather than replace ideas with your own. If you have concerns about any risks attached to the delegated task, then you should set up further coaching sessions at specified stages in the project before important decisions are made. During those sessions your comments should be informative rather than directive.

98 Coach your successor to assume a managerial role.

99 Assume everyone can be a manager, unless it is proven otherwise.

EMPOWERING THROUGH DELEGATION

STAFF BENEFITS   **MANAGER BENEFITS**

Staff are empowered and challenged

DELEGATE WORK
Assign responsibility for part of your own work

More time for concentrating on leadership

Staff are motivated by their own decisions

STEP BACK
Resist the urge to control, so staff can form their own approach

More time to manage and less stress incurred

Staff retain initiative but benefit from support

MONITOR RISKS
Answer questions, make suggestions, assess progress

Risk of failure can be recognized and acted on

Staff enjoy success and an enhanced reputation

REVIEW SUCCESS
Give constructive feedback, and praise good results

Successful results are a reflection of good management

REINFORCING LEARNING

When you integrate delegation opportunities into your coaching work, follow up by asking about what has been learned during work on a project. On completion of the work, arrange for a meeting with the employee in order to discuss how the individual has developed as a result of their involvement on the project. Make links between these achievements and those needed on other assignments. Establish what new knowledge and skills were acquired as a result and how these can be used in future work.

100 Call a meeting to review what has been learned.

101 Identify proven strengths in your staff.

QUESTIONS TO ASK YOURSELF

Q Which responsibilities am I hanging on to for fear of appearing not to be "in charge?"

Q How would I like my manager to coach me to take on more responsibility?

Q Have I delegated interesting and rewarding jobs?

EXAMINING ATTITUDES

The hallmark of a first-class coach is often summed up in their attitude to delegation. Poor coaches see delegation as a way to make life easier for themselves, while retaining control. Good coaches use coaching as a means of developing people even though this may mean taking risks and spending more time supporting personnel. Look honestly at your own attitudes and question any limiting beliefs you may have about human potential.

COACHING TO LEAD

Good coaches want to help people develop because, in the long run, they know that this will enable them to develop their leadership skills, rather than just managing. The manager focuses on running things well; a leader focuses on innovation. Leaders have an obvious interest in coaching and delegating because these are the means through which they can move from being a manager to being a leader.

SHOWING GOOD LEADERSHIP ▶
If you have a positive attitude to your staff and to delegating, you can concentrate on getting the best results for your organization. Give staff your support and encouragement.

ASSESSING YOUR COACHING SKILLS

*E*valuate your performance as a coach by responding to the following statements, and mark the option that is closest to your experience. Be as honest as you can: if your answer is "never," mark Option 1; if it is "always," mark Option 4, and so on. Add your scores together, and refer to the Analysis to see how you scored. Use your answers to identify areas that need most improvement.

OPTIONS
1 Never
2 Occasionally
3 Frequently
4 Always

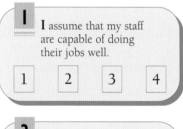

1 I assume that my staff are capable of doing their jobs well.

1 2 3 4

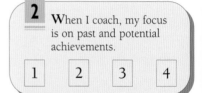

2 When I coach, my focus is on past and potential achievements.

1 2 3 4

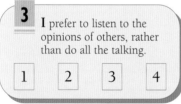

3 I prefer to listen to the opinions of others, rather than do all the talking.

1 2 3 4

4 I am ready to receive negative feedback from my team members.

1 2 3 4

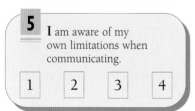

5 I am aware of my own limitations when communicating.

1 2 3 4

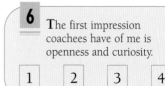

6 The first impression coachees have of me is openness and curiosity.

1 2 3 4

7 I seek to involve staff in making important decisions on a project.

1 | 2 | 3 | 4

8 I treat my staff as partners rather than subordinates.

1 | 2 | 3 | 4

9 My coaching sessions are free of interruptions and distractions.

1 | 2 | 3 | 4

10 I am flexible in switching between discussing goals and exploring problems.

1 | 2 | 3 | 4

11 I believe that people will exercise responsibility when empowered to do so.

1 | 2 | 3 | 4

12 I make links between my staff's motivational needs and their goals.

1 | 2 | 3 | 4

13 I seek to establish what is at the heart of my employee's concerns.

1 | 2 | 3 | 4

14 I am alert to small nonverbal clues when interpreting communication.

1 | 2 | 3 | 4

15 I presuppose that everybody has underutilized strengths and talents.

1 | 2 | 3 | 4

16 I summarize and reflect on what is said in order to check mutual understanding.

1 | 2 | 3 | 4

17 I assume that positive changes can be simple to achieve.

1 2 3 4

18 I prefer to ask open-ended questions rather than closed ones.

1 2 3 4

19 I am not afraid to coach my superiors and colleagues as well as my staff.

1 2 3 4

20 I believe good communication is based on seeing different views.

1 2 3 4

21 When coaching, I assume that my staff can find their own solutions.

1 2 3 4

22 I believe that some of the best coaching results come from creative insight.

1 2 3 4

23 When I give feedback on weak performance, I am constructive and specific.

1 2 3 4

24 I close coaching sessions by getting a specific commitment to a task.

1 2 3 4

25 I control coaching sessions by linking what has been said to the goal.

1 2 3 4

26 I follow up coaching by asking for briefings on progress.

1 2 3 4

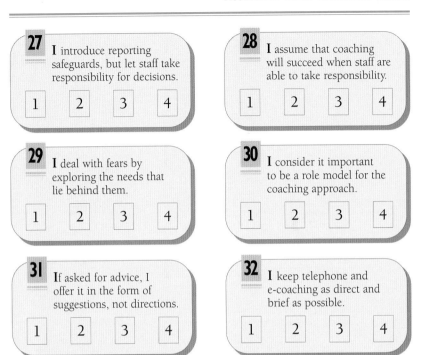

27 I introduce reporting safeguards, but let staff take responsibility for decisions.

1 2 3 4

28 I assume that coaching will succeed when staff are able to take responsibility.

1 2 3 4

29 I deal with fears by exploring the needs that lie behind them.

1 2 3 4

30 I consider it important to be a role model for the coaching approach.

1 2 3 4

31 If asked for advice, I offer it in the form of suggestions, not directions.

1 2 3 4

32 I keep telephone and e-coaching as direct and brief as possible.

1 2 3 4

ANALYSIS

Now you have completed the self-assessment, add up your total score and check your performance by referring to the corresponding evaluation below. Identify your weakest areas, and refer to the relevant sections in this book to develop and hone your coaching skills.
32–64: There are many skills that you need to practice in order to be a successful coach. Work on your personal attitudes to coaching values, as well as specific skills.

37–48: You have reasonable coaching skills, but certain areas require improvement. Focus on improvement in the areas of your test where you scored low marks.
96–128: You are a successful coach, but do not become complacent. Keep striving to get the best from your team, and to develop coaching values in others.

INDEX

ACKNOWLEDGMENTS

AUTHOR'S ACKNOWLEDGMENTS

This book owes its existence to the vision, help, and guidance of Stephanie Jackson and Adèle Hayward at Dorling Kindersley. Many thanks also to Kate Hayward and Laura Watson at Studio Cactus for their fine design work and innovative solutions. We owe much to the many stimulating writers on management upon whose work we have drawn and would like to mention in particular, John Nicholls, for his ideas on delegation and empowerment. We are also indebted, for their support and ideas in developing our approach to coaching, to Paul King, Jane Slemeck, and Yvonne Eaton. We could not have done it without you.

PUBLISHER'S ACKNOWLEDGMENTS

Dorling Kindersley would like to thank the following for their help and participation:

Editorial Daphne Richardson, Mark Wallace;
Indexer Hilary Bird; **Proofreader** Polly Boyd; **Photography** Gary Ombler.

Models Roger André, Philip Argent, Clare Borg, Angela Cameron, Kuo Kang Chen, Russell Cosh, Patrick Dobbs, Carole Evans, Vosjava Fahkro, John Gillard, Kate Hayward, Richard Hill, Cornell John, Maggie Mant, Frankie Mayers, Sotiris Melioumis, Karen Murray, Chantal Newall, Matsumi Niwa, Kiran Shah, Lois Sharland, Lynne Staff, Peter Taylor, Wendy Yun; **Make-up** Jane Hope-Kavanagh.

Picture researcher Franziska Marking; **Picture librarian** Melanie Simmonds, Denise O'Brien

PICTURE CREDITS

The publisher would like to thank the following for their kind permission to reproduce their photographs:

Key: b=bottom; c=center; l=left; r=right; t=top
Empics Ltd: Steve Lipofsky 45tr; Tony Marshall 14tr;
Powerstock Photolibrary / Zefa: 6bl;
Sporting Pictures (UK) Ltd: 56bl;
Tony Stone Images: Walter Hodges 29tr;
Superstock Ltd: 4–5tr; **Telegraph Colour Library**: Rob Brimson 55br

AUTHOR'S BIOGRAPHY

Dr. John Eaton PhD is a founder and director of Coaching Solutions, an innovative company offering executive coaching and training programs in coaching skills to blue-chip concerns throughout the UK. He contributes regularly to journals such as *Theory and Psychology*, *Organisations and People*, and *Changes and Training Journal*. He is also, with Roy Johnson, the author of *Business Applications of NLP: 30 Activities for Training*.

Roy Johnson MBA is a founder and director of Coaching Solutions and is also Director of Pace an award-winning management and sales training company with a wide variety of medium- to large-sized clients. He is the author of *40 Activities for Training in NLP* and co-author of *Business Applications of NLP: 30 Activities for Training*. He and John Eaton have recently launched their new online coaching skills training service on www.coachskills.com